FOOD OF NAPLES

JOHNNY DI FRANCESCO

FOOD OF NAPLES

authentic Neapolitan cuisine

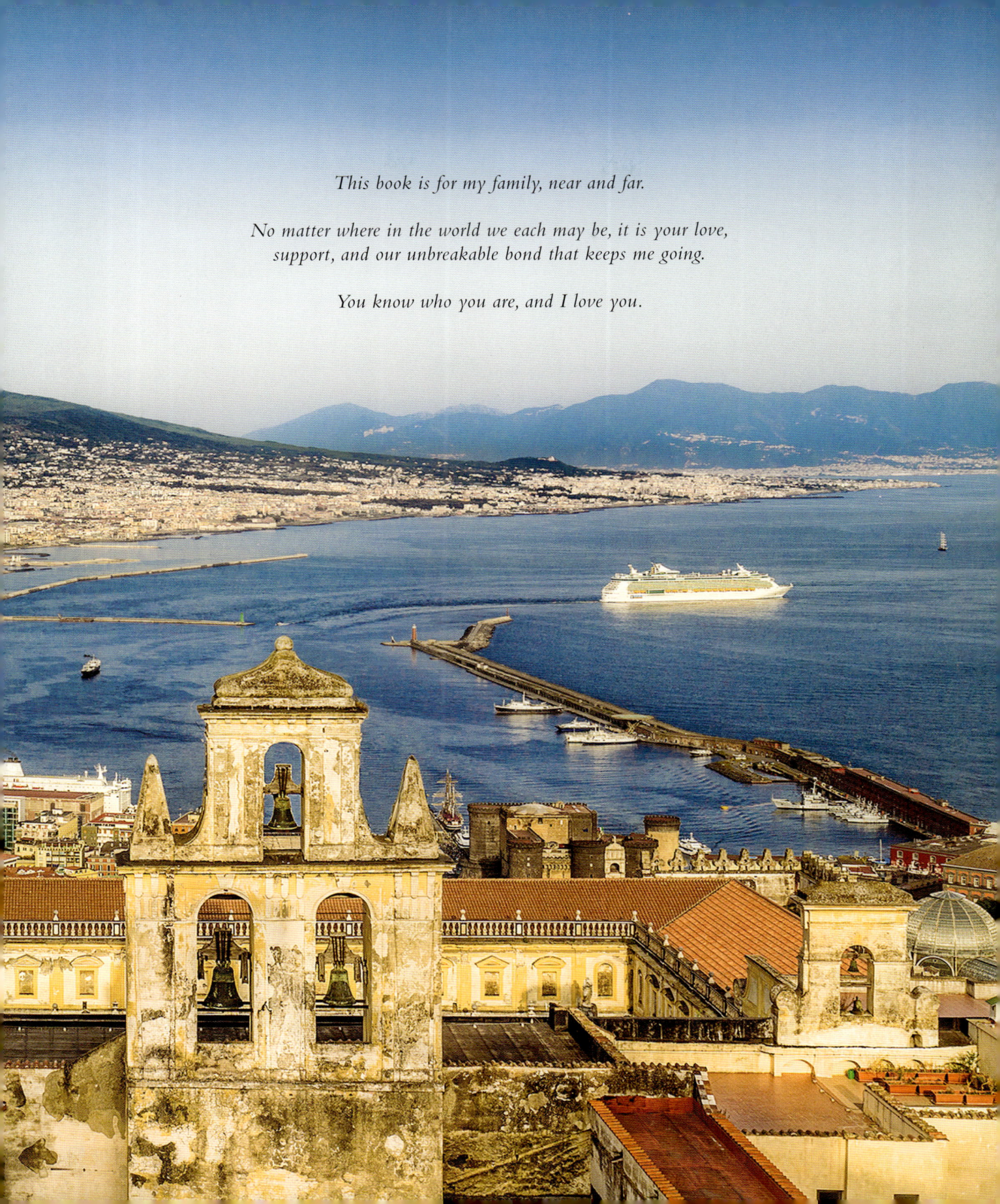

This book is for my family, near and far.

No matter where in the world we each may be, it is your love, support, and our unbreakable bond that keeps me going.

You know who you are, and I love you.

Contents

INTRODUCTION 8

1 CONTORNI E ANTIPASTI 13
Starters & Side Dishes

2 PRESERVE 37
Preserves

3 PASTA E RISOTTI 47
Pasta & Risotto

4 PESCE E CARNE 75
Fish & Meat

5 DOLCI 93
Desserts

6 INSALATA 105
Salad

7 IL CAPITOLO FONDAMENTALE 115
Basics

INDEX 140

INTRODUCTION

Mention Naples and it is difficult for me to remain present in whatever conversation was just taking place. My mind immediately drifts to a place that is a second home - the home of my family for generations, and a place of great joy today for my own family. For me Naples means roots, history, love, tradition, and of course food.

Beautiful, vibrant, and full of incredible contrasts, Naples is more than a jumping off point to the Amalfi Coast. Naples is a place steeped in history – *my* history – and it's of course the birthplace of the original Neapolitan pizza, without which I wouldn't be writing this book, nor would you be holidng it in your hands.

Neapolitan pizza is an incredibly special thing, particularly for me, and many people travel to Naples purely to sate their appetite for traditional pizza in its birthplace. But the food scene in Naples is about more than just pizza, and although traditional Neapolitan pizza has carved my career as a Chef, just like the city of Naples, my restaurants are also about more than just great traditional pizza – they're about all the wonderful facets of Italian food.

Italian food means so many things to so many people – the sheer variety of it almost defies its abiility to be grouped as just 'Italian'. Italian cuisine varies dramatically by region, although there is no denying that there are strong influences that weave through all. For me, Naples is where I find most of my food inspiration. Neapolitan cuisine is a source of joy for me. It brings family and friends together like few other things, and many of the dishes I cook regularly are a source of comfort – not just due to the nature of the food itself, but because of the obvious link it has to my history.

One of my favourite things about food from Naples is the variety of flavours, textures, and techniques that the area is famed for - a result of the influence of different cultures that have controlled the area over time, including Spain, France, the Greeks and the Romans. Much of the cuisine of the region comes from the traditions of the Campania region which used regional ingredients and seafood – both of which are still found in abundance throughout restaurants in Naples today.

The ability of the providors and restauranteurs in Naples to continually blend the tradition and history of the regions food with modern day influences is nothing short of inspirational. The commitment of the entire area and its people to preserving its heritage is one that I share, and it's a heritage that I pass on to my own family through not only the food that I make, but by ensuring our history is woven into our current lives.

There's a good reason that Naples is often called an open-air museum, and like any good museum, I definitely learn something new every time I return. I try to bring that blend of new and old into my cooking. I work hard to keep tradition sacred, but just like they are doing in the kitchens of Naples I experiment with new flavours and ways to keep those traditions relevant. I have always wanted to bring a real taste of Naples to Australia, so I hope that people who eat my food perceive it for what it is – traditional Neapolitan cuisine.

In the following pages you will find some of my favourite dishes - dishes that have been inspired by my frequent trips back to the city from which my family hails; dishes that I have discovered wandering the streets of Naples, being drawn into a tiny restaurant made known only by the incredible aromas filtering into the air as you pass by. This is the Naples that I know and love – the Naples that is filled with amazing food, and people who are passionate about making it.

CONTORNI E ANTIPASTI

Starters & Side Dishes

POLPETTE

Meatballs

1 kg (2 lb 4 oz) minced (ground) beef
1 egg
1 garlic clove, grated
15 g (½ oz) salt
black pepper, to taste
30 g (1 oz) grated parmesan cheese
pinch of oregano
200 ml (7 fl oz) milk
50 g (1¾ oz) breadcrumbs
¼ bunch freshly chopped parsley
Napoli sauce, to serve (see page 123)

SERVES 4 / MAKES APPROX. 12 MEATBALLS

Preheat the oven to 220°C (425°F). Line a baking tray with baking paper.

Place all of the ingredients in a large mixing bowl. Mix well using your hands. Roll the mixture into balls (about 100 g/3½ oz each). Wet your palm with a drop of water to help with the rolling.

Place each ball on the baking paper and bake for approximately 20 minutes.

In a pot, heat the Napoli sauce over medium heat. Carefully place the meatballs in the pot and continue to cook over low heat for 45 minutes. Serve hot with toasted bread.

-Starters & Side Dishes-

ARANCINI

Bolognese filling
1 garlic clove, chopped
1 onion, diced
⅓ carrot, diced
100 g (3½ oz) peas
1 celery stalk, diced
2 kg (4 lb 8 oz) minced (ground) beef
100 ml (3½ fl oz) red wine
1.5 l (52 fl oz) crushed tomatoes (pelati)
1 bay leaf
⅓ fresh rosemary stalk
salt flakes and pepper, to taste

Risotto mixture
1 tablespoon olive oil
½ onion
1 kg (2 lb 4 oz) arborio rice
125 ml (4 fl oz) white wine
1 l (35 fl oz) chicken or vegetable stock
50 g (1¾ oz) grated parmesan
salt and pepper, to taste

Crumbing
2 eggs
250 ml (9 fl oz) milk
100 g (3½ oz) plain (all-purpose) flour
500 g (1 lb 2 oz) fine breadcrumbs

60g (2¼ oz) mozzarella
500 ml (17 fl oz) vegetable oil
rose sauce, to serve (see page 120)

SERVES 4—6 PEOPLE / MAKES APPROX. 20 ARANCINI BALLS

To make the bolognese filling, sauté the garlic in a large saucepan over medium heat. Add the onions, carrot and celery then cook until golden brown. Add the minced (ground) beef and cook for 15–20 minutes, then add the red wine and keep cooking for 15–20 minutes. Add the crushed tomato and bay leaves and when it starts to boil, reduce the heat to low and simmer for 1½ hours. Add the peas 20 minutes before the sauce is finished. Add the rosemary, salt flakes and pepper. Mix well. Remove from the heat and transfer to a bowl. Allow to cool.

To make the risotto mixture, heat the olive oil in a large saucepan over medium heat. Add the onion, and cook, stirring until onion is soft but not browned. Pour in the rice, and cook stirring for 2 minutes, then deglaze with the white wine, and continue cooking and stirring until the liquid has evaporated. Add hot chicken or vegetable stock to the rice 80 ml (2½ fl oz) at a time, stirring and cooking until the liquid has evaporated before adding more. When the chicken or vegetable stock has all been added, and the liquid has evaporated turn heat off and transfer the rice into a bowl, add the parmesan, salt, pepper and mix in well, gentle to avoid breaking and of the rice grains.

To make the crumbing, in a small bowl, whisk together the eggs and milk with a fork. Pour the flour and breadcrumbs in separate bowls and set aside.

Shape the risotto mix into balls (about 100 g/3½ oz). Make a well in the center: add 1 teaspoon of

the bolognese filling and a small cube of mozzarella. Close the well by squeezing the rice into a ball.

Lightly coat the risotto ball with flour, dip into the milk mixture before rolling it in the breadcrumbs to coat.

Heat the oil for frying in a deep-fryer or large deep saucepan to 175°C (347°F). Fry the balls in small batches until evenly golden, turning as needed. Drain on paper towels. Keep warm in a low oven while the rest are frying. Serve with rose sauce (see page 120).

BOCCONCINI

Bocconcini

80 ml (2½ fl oz) extra virgin olive oil
1 garlic clove, finely sliced
1 yellow capsicum (pepper), diced
1 red capsicum (pepper), diced
12 pitted black Taggiasca olives
12 capers
6 slices thin slices of parma ham
12 large basil leaves, plus extra for garnish
300 g (10½ oz) buffalo bocconcini
   (fresh baby mozzarella cheese)

SERVES 6

Preheat the oven to 200°C (400°F).

Grease a baking tray.

Heat a saucepan over high heat. Add the oil, garlic and capsicum and sauté until caramelized. Add the olives and capers, then remove from the heat and set aside.

Lay the slices of ham on the bench. Place a basil leaf and bocconcini ¾ of the length of the ham and wrap the ham around.

Place the ham on the baking tray and bake for 5 minutes, or until the mozzarella just starts to melt.

To serve, arrange a serving plate with the capsicum mixture and place the wrapped bocconcini on top. Garnish with basil leaves.

Note: This is a great entrée to start the evening.

Starters & Side Dishes

FUNGHI RIPIENI

Stuffed mushrooms

6 large cup mushrooms
zest and juice of 1 lemon
20 ml (¾ fl oz) olive oil
½ onion, finely chopped
20 ml (¾ fl oz) white wine
20 g (¾ oz) breadcrumbs
1 egg
salt and pepper, to taste
20 g (¾ oz) grated parmesan cheese
5 g (⅕ oz) flat-leaf (Italian) parsley, finely chopped

SERVES 6 / MAKES 6

Preheat the oven to 180°C (350°F).

Grease a baking tray.

Clean the mushrooms thoroughly. Pull each mushroom stalk out and set aside. Carefully peel the mushroom outer skin from the entire mushroom. Rub with lemon juice and set aside. The lemon will keep the mushroom from turning brown. Cut the stalks into small cubes.

Heat the olive oil in a frying pan over medium heat. Add the onion and simmer until transparent. Add the chopped mushroom stalks. Cook for 2 minutes, then deglaze with the white wine. Cook until the onion and mushroom stalks are tender. Remove from the heat.

Place the cooked onion and mushroom in a bowl. Add the breadcrumbs, some lemon zest, parsley, egg and salt and pepper to taste. Mix gently to combine.

Place the mushrooms onto the baking tray and spoon the filling into each mushroom. Top with grated parmesan.

Bake for 20–30 minutes, or until the parmesan turns golden brown.

Serve hot.

Starters & Side Dishes

FIORI DI ZUCCA RIPIENI DI GRANCHIO

Zucchini flowers with crab filling

Crab filling

100 g (3½ oz) crabmeat
350 g (12 oz) ricotta cheese, strained through a drum sieve
10 g (¼ oz) grated parmesan cheese
5 g (⅛ oz) chopped flat-leaf (Italian) parsley
5 g (⅛ oz) breadcrumbs
pinch of salt
½ egg
zest of 1 lemon
500 ml (17 fl oz) vegetable oil

Batter

250 ml (9 fl oz) soda water
60 ml (2 fl oz) rice flour
60 ml (2 fl oz) plain (all-purpose) flour

500 ml (17 fl oz) vegetable oil, for frying
12 zucchini flowers

SERVES 6—12 / MAKES 12

To make the crab filling, combine all of the ingredients in a large bowl and mix together well. Transfer the mixture to a piping bag.

Clean each zucchini flower and remove the internal stem. Once cleaned, pipe the mixture into each flower (about 45 g/1½ oz of filling). Close the top of the flower and set aside.

To make the batter, add the soda water to a bowl and mix in the rice flour and plain flour.

Heat the oil in a deep-fryer or large deep saucepan to 175°C (347°F).

Dip each flower in the batter, one by one. Carefully place each zucchini flower in the fryer. Fry in small batches until evenly golden, turning as needed. Drain on paper towels.

-Starters & Side Dishes-

MELANZANE ALLA PARMIGIANA

Eggplant parmigiana

700 g (1 lb 9 oz) sliced eggplant (aubergine), 5 mm/¼ in thickness
plain (all-purpose) flour, to dust
500 ml (17 fl oz) vegetable oil, for frying
1 l (35 fl oz) Napoli sauce (see page 123)
300 g (10½ oz) grated parmesan cheese
500 g (1 lb 2 oz) buffalo ricotta cheese
25 basil leaves
300 g (10½ oz) fine breadcrumbs
2 balls buffalo mozzarella cheese

SERVES 6

Lightly salt the sliced eggplant and leave on a wire rack to rest for 1 hour.

Dry the eggplants, then dust evenly with the flour. Heat the oil in a deep-fryer or large deep saucepan to 175°C (347°F). Deep-fry the eggplant until golden, then set aside to cool.

Preheat the oven to 180°C (350°F). Place a small amount of Napoli sauce in a terracotta dish. Layer the eggplant, breadcrumbs, Napoli sauce, parmesan, ricotta and basil. Repeat the process twice more.

Top with buffalo mozzarella, then cover with baking paper and foil. Place in the oven and cook the parmigiana for 30 minutes. Serve hot.

CARPACCIO DI MANZO

Beef carpaccio

300 g (10½ oz) girello (silverside)
salt and pepper, to taste
2 whole marinated artichokes, thinly sliced
100 g (3½ oz) shaved parmesan cheese
20 g (¾ oz) rocket (arugula) leaves
150 ml (5 fl oz) lemon dressing (see page 128)

SERVES 6—8

Clean any sinew from the girello. Tightly wrap in plastic wrap and freeze for approximately 30 minutes (this will help with the slicing).

Thinly slice the Girello and neatly arrange around two plates. Season the girello with salt and pepper.

Arrange the sliced artichokes over the girello. Top with the parmesan and rocket. Drizzle with the lemon dressing and serve.

COZZE RIPIENE

Stuffed mussels

36 mussels
20 ml (¾ fl oz) tablespoons olive oil
1 onion, finely chopped
24 capers, rinsed
1 tablespoon white wine
20 g (¾ oz) breadcrumbs
zest of 1 lemon
1 egg
salt and pepper, to taste
20 g (¾ oz) grated parmesan cheese
5 g (⅕ oz) flat-leaf (Italian) parsley, finely chopped

MAKES 36

Preheat the oven to 180°C (350°F).

Clean the mussels thoroughly. Scrub the mussels and pull out the hairy beards. Discard any broken mussels, or open ones that don't close when tapped on the bench. Rinse well. When cooked, discard any unopened mussels.

Place the olive oil and mussels into a pan over medium heat, allowing the oil and mussels to heat at the same time. Cover the pan to create some steam. This can take up to 5 minutes. You will notice the mussels open and release their juices. Remove from the heat and transfer the mussels to a baking tray using tongs. You can also use a steam pot to steam the mussels.

In a separate pan, add some olive oil and preheat gently. Add the onion and simmer until transparent.

Add the capers and cook for 2 minutes, then deglaze with the white wine. Cook until the onion and capers are tender. Remove from the heat.

Transfer the cooked onion and capers to a bowl and add the breadcrumbs, lemon zest, parsley egg and salt and pepper to taste. Mix gently to combine. Avoid over-mixing, you don't want to create a paste.

Fill each mussel with the mixture. Top with the parmesan.

Bake for 10–15 minutes, or until the parmesan turns golden brown. Garnish with the parsley.

Serve hot or cold.

-Starters & Side Dishes-

POLIPETTI AFFOGATI

Drowned baby octopus

1.5 kg (3 lb 5 oz) fresh baby octopus
100 g (3½ oz) extra virgin olive oil olive oil
750 g (1 lb 10 oz) peeled tomato
1 fresh chilli, finely sliced
70 g (2½ oz) black Gaeta olives
30 g (1 oz) baby capers
2 handfuls chopped flat-leaf (Italian) parsley
salt, to taste

SERVES 6

To clean the octopus, use a small knife and carefully cut between the head and tentacles of the octopus, just below the eyes. Grasp the body of the octopus and push the beak out and up through the center of the tentacles with your finger. Cut the eyes from the head of the octopus by slicing a small disc off with a sharp knife. Discard the eye section. To clean the octopus head, carefully slit through one side, avoiding the ink sac and scrape out the inside. Rinse under running water to remove any remaining grit.

Add all the ingredients, except the parsley, to a large pot (preferably a terracotta pot). Cover the pot with baking paper, then cover with the lid. Bring to the boil over medium heat, then reduce the heat to low and cook for 45 minutes.

Check the consistency of the dish. If the liquid is still runny, remove the octopus and reduce the liquid to a dark, shiny consistency. Return the octopus to the dish and warm for 3 minutes. Just before serving, garnish with the parsley.

Note: As the capers and olives may add flavor while cooking, ensure you taste for salt.

-Starters & Side Dishes-

FRITELLE DI BACCALA

Salt cod fritters

Poached eggs
1.5 l (52 fl oz) water
100 ml (3½ fl oz) white wine vinegar, for poaching
6 eggs

Lemon garlic sauce
1 l (35 fl oz) milk
10 garlic cloves
½ tablespoon dijon mustard
300 ml (10½ fl oz) olive oil
100 ml (3½ fl oz) lemon juice
zest of 1 lemon
½ tablespoon Worcestershire sauce
½ tablespoon white wine vinegar
salt and pepper, to taste

250 g (9 oz) 00 flour
4 g (⅛ oz) dried yeast
salt, to taste
200 ml (7 fl oz) warm water
500 g (1 lb 2 oz) hydrated salted cod (bacala)
1 l (35 fl oz) oil, for frying
1 bunch flat-leaf (Italian) parsley
3 anchovies
300 ml (10½ fl oz) soy oil

SERVES 6—12

To poach the eggs, add the water and vinegar to a pot. Bring to the boil over medium heat. In a separate bowl, crack open each egg. Gently add the eggs to the boiling water, turn the water to simmer and cook the eggs to a soft poach. Remove the eggs with a slotted spoon.

To make the lemon garlic sauce, add half the milk and all the garlic to a small pot. Bring to the boil over medium heat, then simmer for 5 minutes. Sieve the garlic and repeat with the remaining milk. Cook until the garlic is soft. In a blender, add the soft poached garlic, dijon mustard and the soft poached eggs while still warm. Process until smooth. Slowly add the olive oil while processing on medium to low speed. Once all the oil has been absorbed, add the lemon juice and zest, Worcestershire Sauce, anchovies, soy oil and vinegar. Season with salt and pepper, to taste.

In a bowl, mix the flour, yeast and salt with the warm water, creating a creamy consistency. Mix well by hand. Leave the mixture to rise in a warm place until it doubles in size.

In the meantime, blanch the salted cod in boiling water without salt for approximately 15 minutes. Remove the salted cod and allow it to reach room temperature. Add the salted cod to the dough mix. Add the parsley.

Preheat the oil in a frying pan over high heat. Once the oil is hot, using a spoon, scoop the mixture of salted cod and add to the oil. Fry until golden. Remove from the fryer and salt and pepper to taste and serve with the lemon garlic sauce.

Note: Type 00 flour is also known as 'dopio zero flour' or 'tipo 00' flour. It has a finer grain than commercial plain flours, resulting in airy, light bread and soft, delicate pasta. You can find it in some supermarkets and specialty food stores.

Starters & Side Dishes

CAPONATA

Caponata

220 g (7¾ oz) eggplants (aubergines), diced and seasoned with 20 g (¾ oz) salt
80 ml (2½ fl oz) olive oil
5 g (⅛ oz) garlic, sliced (½ garlic clove)
65 g (2¼ oz) onion, diced
180 g (6½ oz) zucchini (courgette), sliced into 1 cm (½ in) discs
90 g (3¼ oz) celery, sliced
80 g (2¾ oz) roasted cherry tomatoes
60 g (2¼ oz) green olives
30 g (1 oz) toasted pinenuts
30 g (1 oz) sultanas
1 tablespoon chardonnay vinegar
10 g (¼ oz) sugar
salt, to taste
torn basil leaves, to garnish

SERVES 6

Salt the eggplant and set aside for 2 hours. Strain and squeeze out the excess water.

Heat the olive oil in a large saucepan over high heat. Add the garlic and onion and fry for 3–4 minutes. Add the zucchini, eggplant and celery and cook for a further 4–5 minutes.

Add the tomatoes and cook for 3 minutes. Add the olives, pinenuts and sultanas and cook for 1 minute.

Combine the vinegar, sugar and salt until dissolved. Add to the caponata mix and cook until the liquid has been absorbed.

Serve cold or hot.

-Starters & Side Dishes-

INSALATA DI MARE

Seafood salad

1.8 kg (4 lb) mussels
1 kg (2 lb 4 oz) clams
600 g (1 lb 5 oz) calamari (squid)
600 g (1 lb 5 oz) prawns (shrimp)
100 ml (3½ fl oz) extra virgin olive oil
2 garlic cloves, finely chopped
2 teaspoons dijon mustard
50 ml (1¾ fl oz) lemon juice
flat-leaf (Italian) parsley, to garnish
salt and pepper, to taste

SERVES 6

Scrub the mussels and pull out the hairy beards. Discard any broken mussels, or open ones that don't close when tapped on the bench. Rinse well. When cooked, discard any unopened mussels.

In a shallow pot add 10ml water with the mussels and clams. Cover the pot with a lid and steam until the mussels and clams are open, this should take no longer than 3–5 minutes. When all the shellfish are open, remove from the pot. Sieve the juice from the shellfish and add into a clean boiling pot. Bring the juices to the boil. If there isn't enough juice to completely cover the calamari, add some water.

Clean and cut the calamari into rings and add to the pot with the juices from the shellfish. Wait until it the liquid reaches boiling point again and remove the calamari from the juices with a slotted spoon.

Bring the same juice to the boil again. Add the prawns with the shell and head. Bring the juice to the boil, then remove the prawns. Place the prawns into an iced bath to cool immediately. Once cool, remove the prawn head, clean the shell and remove the internal vein.

Place all of the seafood into a salad bowl. Dress with the remaining ingredients and season with salt and pepper, to taste. Serve in iceberg lettuce cups.

Tip: You may like to add chilli.

—Starters & Side Dishes—

PRESERVE 2

Preserves

TONNO SOTT'OLIO

Tuna in oil

1 kg (2 lb 4 oz) cleaned fresh tuna
1.5 l (52 fl oz) water
500 ml (17 fl oz) white wine vinegar
300 g (10½ oz) rock salt
2 bay leaves
1 star anise
1 cinnamon stick
zest and juice of 1 lemon
10 peppercorns
olive oil (enough to fill the jars)

SERVES 4 / MAKES APPROX. 5 SMALL JARS

Place all of the ingredients, except the olive oil and tuna, into a pot over medium heat. Bring to the boil.

Cut the cleaned tuna into five 200 g (7 oz) pieces. Add to the boiling pot and simmer for approximately 5 minutes, or until cooked in the center.

Drain the tuna in a colander covered with a clean cloth and allow to cool to room temperature. Add the cooked tuna to glass jars and cover completely with the olive oil.

Close with the jar lid, then place in a pot. Cover with water and bring to boiling point slowly. Simmer for 5 minutes. Turn the heat off and allow the water to cool with the jars in the water.

Tips: Only add tuna to the jars, no other ingredients. Do not remove the jars from the boiling water as this may cause the jar to crack.

SARDINE SOTT'OLIO

Sardines in oil

1.5 l (52 fl oz) water
500 ml (17 fl oz) white wine vinegar
300 g (10½ oz) rock salt
2 bay leaves
1 star anise
1 cinnamon stick
10 peppercorns
1 kg (2 lb 4 oz) sardines
olive oil (enough to fill the jars)

Marinade
100 ml (3½ fl oz) extra virgin olive oil
500 g (1 lb 2 oz) onions, diced
100 g (3½ oz) capers
½ teaspoon nutmeg
2 bay leaves
1 star anise
1 cinnamon stick
1 lemon zest
white pepper, to taste
salt, to taste

SERVES 4 / MAKES APPROX. 5 SMALL JARS

To make the marinade, add all the ingredients in a pot over medium heat, bring to a simmer and cook the onion until translucent and soft. Set aside until needed.

Place the water, white wine vinegar, rock salt, bay leaves, star anise, cinnamon stick and peppercorns into a pot. Bring to the boil.

Add all the sardines at once to the boiling pot and simmer for approximately 5 minutes or until cooked in the center.

Drain the sardines in a colander covered with a clean cloth and allow to cool to room temperature. Once cooled, fillet each sardine.

Add the cooked sardines to the jars in layers, with the marinade between each layer. Cover completely with the olive oil. Once all the jars are covered, seal with the jar lid.

Place the jars in a pot, cover with water and bring the water to boiling point slowly, then simmer for 5 minutes. Turn the heat off and allow the water to cool with the jars in the water.

Tip: Do not remove the jars from the boiling water as this may cause the jar to crack.

MELANZANE SOTT'OLIO

Eggplant in oil

5 kg (10 lb 4 oz) eggplant (aubergine)
rock salt (enough to cover eggplant)

2 l (70 fl oz) white wine vinegar
2–3 garlic cloves
1 fresh chilli, finely sliced
750 g (1 lb 10 oz) extra virgin oil
oregano, to taste

SERVES 4—6 PEOPLE PER JAR / MAKES APPROX. 25 JARS

Peel the eggplant and cut into strips. Place the cut eggplant in a colander and cover with rock salt. Leave for 2 hours, at room temperature. Wash all the salt from the eggplant and squeeze as much liquid as you can from the eggplant.

Add the vinegar to a pot and bring to the boil. Add the eggplant and bring to the boil. Drain the eggplant in a colander and allow to cool. Squeeze as much water as possible from the cooked eggplant. Dress the eggplant with the remaining ingredients.

Add the eggplants to a jar and cover with the oil, ensuring that the oil sits at least 1 cm (¾ in) above the eggplant.

Tips: The eggplants are best eaten after 1 month. Do not remove the jars from the boiling water as this may cause the jar to crack, allow the water to cool first.

GADINIERA SOTT'OLIO

Pickled vegetables in oil

1 kg (2 lb 4 oz) baby carrots (mixed color)
1 kg (2 lb 4 oz) cauliflower
1 kg (2 lb 4 oz) baby capsicum (pepper)
1 kg (2 lb 4 oz) baby turnip
1 kg (2 lb 4 oz) baby beetroot
rock salt (enough to salt all the vegetables)
2 l (70 fl oz) white wine vinegar
750 g (1 lb 10 oz) extra virgin oil

SERVES 4—6 PEOPLE PER JAR / MAKES APPROX. 25 JARS

Brush all the skin off the baby carrots. Cut the cauliflower in to small pieces. If the turnip and beetroot are small leave them as is. If they are over 2 cm (¾ in) in diameter, cut in half or quarters.

Salt all the vegetables separately for a minimum of 6 hours.

Add the vinegar to a pot and bring to the boil over medium heat. Add the vegetables in order from the lightest to darkest, cooking each ingredient seperately. Drain each vegetable into a colander allow to cool.

Add the vegetables to the jar in color harmony and cover with the oil, ensuring that the oil sits at least 1 cm (¾ in) above the vegetables.

Once all the jars are covered, seal with the jar lid. Place the jars in a pot, cover with water and bring the water to boiling point slowly, then simmer for 5 minutes. Turn the heat off and allow the water to cool with the jars in the water.

Tip: Do not remove the jars from the boiling water as this may cause the jar to crack.

3

PASTA E RISOTTI

Pasta & Risotto

MALTAGLIATI CON COZZE E PEPERONI

Maltagliati with mussels and capsicum

2 garlic cloves
1 chilli, chopped
150 ml (5 fl oz) extra virgin olive oil
1.5kg (3 lb 5 oz) mussels
250 ml (9 fl oz) white wine
fresh pasta recipe (see page 117)
600 g (1 lb 5 oz) off-cuts from fresh pasta (if not, cut the fresh pasta in irregular shapes)
300 g (10½ oz) roasted capsicum, peeled
1 thyme sprig
zest of 1 lemon

SERVES 6

Roast the capsicum over a chargrill or bake in an oven until blackened.

In a large pan over medium heat, sauté the garlic and chilli in some oil until golden. Add the mussels and sauté for 1 minute. Add the wine and cook until the mussels are open. Remove from the heat and de-shell all the mussels. Keep 18 mussels in the shell. Keep all the mussels in the juices on the side.

Fill a large pot with salted water and bring to the boil. Add the pasta to the boiling water and cook for approximately 2–3 minutes or until *al dente*.

Meanwhile, in a large sauté pan, warm the roasted capsicum and the thyme with the remaining extra virgin olive oil. Add the mussels and juice and bring all ingredients to a simmer.

Drain the pasta and add to the sauce and emulsify with some extra virgin olive oil to finish off. Plate the pasta and garnish with lemon zest.

PACCHERRI CON GENOVESE DI PIOVRA

Paccherri with Genovese octopus

2 garlic cloves
200 g (7 oz) potato, diced
150 ml (5 fl oz) extra virgin olive oil
800 g (1 lb 12 oz) red onion, sliced
1.2 kg (2 lb 12 oz) fresh large octopus
200 ml (7 fl oz) white wine
200 g (7 oz) cherry tomatoes
salt and white pepper, to taste
600 g (1 lb 5 oz) paccheri pasta
flat-leaf (Italian) parsley, finely chopped, to garnish
zest of 1 lemon

SERVES 6

In a large shallow pot over medium heat, sauté the garlic and potato with the extra virgin olive oil. Once the potato is soft, add the onion and cook until soft.

Cut the fresh octopus into small pieces and add to the pot. Add the wine and cook until the octopus is soft and the onions have broken down.

Add the cherry tomato and salt and pepper and cook for approximately 10 minutes.

In the meantime, bring a large pot of salted water to the boil. Add the pasta and cook for approximately 2 minutes less than the recommended cooking time on the packet. Drain the pasta and retain some of the water for the pot.

Add the pasta to the octopus ragù, cook until the pasta is *al dente* (approximately 2–4 minutes). Add the chopped parsley and lemon zest. Serve hot.

PASTA CON FAGIOLI E COZZE

Pasta with beans and mussels

350 g (12 oz) fagioli
1 l (35 fl oz) water
2 bay leaves
1 onion
1 carrot
2 celery stalks
5 peppercorns
200 g (7 oz) extra virgin olive oil
2 garlic cloves
1.5 kg (3 lb 5 oz) mussels
20 ml (¾ fl oz) white wine
400 g (14 oz) tubetti piccoli pasta
1 handful flat-leaf (Italian) parsley

200 g (7 oz) peeled tomatoes
1 fresh chilli, finely sliced

SERVES 6

To cook the fagioli, add the water to a pot along with the fagioli and allow to soak overnight.

The next day, strain the fagioli and weigh. In a pot, add double the weight of the fagioli in water. Add the bay leaves, half an onion, half a carrot and 1 celery stalk. Add the peppercorns and cook, covered, for about 1½ hours, or until the beans are soft and tender.

Once cooked, divide half the beans. Keep ½ whole and the other ½ purée in a food processor. Set aside until needed.

In a large pan over medium heat, add 50 ml extra virgin olive oil, chilli and sauté the garlic until golden. Add the mussels and sauté for 1 minute. Add the wine and cook until the mussels are open. Remove from the heat and deshell all the mussels. Keep 18 mussels in the shell. Keep all the mussels in the juices on the side.

Bring a pot of salted water to the boil. Add the pasta and cook for approximately half the time specified on the packet. Strain the pasta but keep some of the water on the side.

Meanwhile, in a separate pot, add the remaining chopped onion, celery and carrot. Sauté with the remaining extra virgin olive oil. Cook until nicely caramelized. Add all of the beans, both puréed and whole peeled tomato.

Add the pasta to the beans and stir constantly until creamy, then add all the liquid from the mussels and stir until creamy again. Taste the pasta, in case the pasta is still undercooked, add the reserved water from the pasta and cook until pasta is *al dente* and has a creamy consistency.

Add the mussels, parsley and a little extra virgin olive oil and serve.

PASTA MISTA CON CAVOLFIORE, ACCIUGHE E PINOLI

Pasta mixed with cauliflower, anchovies & pine nuts

100 ml (3½ fl oz) extra virgin olive oil
1 garlic clove, chopped
1 chilli, finely sliced
6 anchovy fillets
600 g (1 lb 5 oz) cauliflower, cut into small florets
salt and pepper, to taste
30 g (1 oz) pine nuts
50 g (1¾ oz) sultanas
1 l (35 fl oz) vegetable stock
500 g (1 lb 2 oz) pasta mista (assorted short pasta)

SERVES 6

Heat the olive oil in a pot over medium heat. Add the garlic, chilli and anchovies and sauté until the anchovies have dissolved. Reduce the heat to low and add the cauliflower and salt and pepper. Cover with a lid and cook until golden and soft.

Add the pinenuts and sultanas and cook for approximately for 5 minutes. Add the vegetable stock and allow to simmer, keep on low heat until the pasta is added.

Meanwhile, bring a pot of salted water to the boil. Add the pasta and cook for approximately half or less than recommended cooking time on the packet. Strain.

Add the pasta to the pot with the sauce and cook until all the vegetable stock has been absorbed and a creamy consistency has formed.

Tip: Retain some of the water from the pasta pot. You can use this to add to the sauce if required.

LINGUINE CON FIORE DI ZUCCHINE, ZUCCHINE E VONGOLE

Linguine with zucchini flowers, zucchini & clams

1.5 kg (3 lb 5 oz) vongole (clams)
150 ml (5 fl oz) extra virgin olive oil
2 garlic cloves
150 ml (5 fl oz) white wine
150 g (5½ oz) zucchini (courgette)
6 zucchini flowers
600 g (1 lb 5 oz) linguine
white pepper, to taste
1 handful flat-leaf (Italian) parsley, finely chopped

SERVES 6

Place the vongole in salted water for 1 hour to clean.

Heat the extra virgin olive oil in a pan over medium heat. Add the garlic and cook until garlic begins to brown. Add the vongole and cover with a lid to steam. Remove the lid and glaze with the white wine. Remove from the heat and de-shell all the vongole except 18.

In the meantime, heat a large pot of salted water over medium heat and bring to the boil.

Cut the zucchini in strips with a mandolin lengthways. Cut the zucchini flowers into quarters.

Add the pasta and cook for approximately 2 minutes less than the recommended cooking time on the packet.

In a sauté pan, add the vongole with the juice and simmer.

Drain the pasta and add to the vongole sauce with the raw zucchini and three-quarters of the zucchini flowers. Add the white pepper and chopped parsley and toss until creamy.

Serve in a large bowl and garnish with the remaining zucchini flowers and parsley.

RAVIOLONI DI GRANCHIO

Crab ravioli with mascarpone and sour tomato sauce

Filling
400 g (14 oz) crab meat (cooked)
200 g (7 oz) mascarpone
1 thyme sprig
zest of 1 lemon
salt and pepper, to taste

600 g (1 lb 5 oz) pasta recipe (see page 117)

Sauce
1 shallot, sliced
1 chilli, sliced
24 cherry tomatoes, halved
100 g (3½ oz) butter
50 ml (1¾ fl oz) lemon juice
100 ml (3½ fl oz) extra virgin olive oil
10 basil leaves
20 mint leaves
1 handful flat-leaf (Italian) parsley

SERVES 6

The best method to roll the pasta is with a pasta rolling machine. Clamp the pasta machine tightly to a table. Divide the dough by 4 with a knife, keep the 4 pieces covered in plastic wrap to avoid drying out. Take one piece at a time and roll it through the machine repetitively by folding the dough at least 3–5 times, until the dough is perfectly rectangular shape to the width of the machine. Start this at the highest setting. Repeat this passing the pasta through the machine on each setting until you reach setting 1. You will have a long, thin pasta sheet.

Place a small ball (approximately 30 g/1 oz) of the crab mix leaving about two finger spaces between each filling. Once you reach the end of the pasta sheet, dividing each filling equally across, dip the brush in water and brush the opposite side of the filling. Fold the brushed side over the filling and push down in between each filling.

Using a ravioli cutter or knife, cut a square around each filling leaving approximately 2 cm (¾ in) around the filling. Once all the ravioli have been cut, press firmly down around the filling removing any air pockets. Repeat this with all the pasta dough until you have used all the filling. (Keep any pasta off-cuts as you can use all of these for the Matagliati pasta recipe.)

Bring a pot of salted water to the boil. Blanch the ravioli and cook until they float to the top of the boiling water (ensure they are soft in the middle). Drain the ravioloni.

To make the sauce, sauté the shallots in a large pan, with the chilli, until transparent. Add the cherry tomatoes and cook until semi-soft. Add the butter and lemon juice.

Once the ravioli are cooked, add them to the sauce. Add the fresh herbs and toss through.

—Pasta & Risotto—

RISOTTO PESCATORE

Seafood risotto

Pescatore Sauce
18 vongole (clams)
18 mussels
60 ml (2 fl oz) extra virgin olive oil
1 garlic clove
1 chilli, finely chopped, to taste
12 large or 16–20 small prawns (shrimp)
12 Canadian scallops
20 ml (¾ fl oz) white wine
150 ml (5 fl oz) fish stock (see page 135)
50 ml (1¾ fl oz) Napoli sauce (see page 123)
10 basil leaves
salt and pepper, to taste

Risotto
50 ml (1¾ fl oz) extra virgin olive oil
1 onion, diced
300 g (10½ oz) Carnaroli rice
150 ml (5 fl oz) white wine
1 l (35 fl oz) fish stock
1 tb unsalted butter
1 handful flat-leaf (Italian) parsley

SERVES 6

Place the vongole in salted water for 1 hour to clean.

To make the pescatore sauce, in a pan add the extra virgin olive oil, garlic and chilli. Cook until the garlic begins to brown, then add the prawns and scallops. Cook for approximately 2 minutes, then add the mussels and vongole. Add the basil. Cover with a lid to steam. Remove the lid and glaze with the white wine. Add fish stock and simmer for 3 minutes approximately, add a touch of Napoli sauce. Set aside until the rice is ready.

To make the risotto, add the extra virgin olive oil to a small pot over medium heat. Sauté the diced onion until transparent. Add the Carnaroli rice and cook over low heat. Once the rice is toasted, add the white wine and wait until wine is fully evaporated. Once the wine has evaporated, add a third of the fish stock and stir until absorbed. Repeat this until all fish stock has been used. Add all the pescatore sauce and cook until a creamy consistency, add remaining fish stock and stir gently on a medium heat consistently. Once the stock has reduced to a creamy consistency take the pot off the heat and add the butter, parsley and stir fast until the butter dissolves. This will add to the creaminess of the risotto.

Tips: Stir with a wooden spoon gently to avoid the rice from breaking. Add the butter. For best results, divide the recipe in two or four pans.

RAVIOLI DI VITELLO CON SALSA DI CARCIOFI

Veal ravioli with artichoke sauce

Sauce
150 g (5½ oz) diced onion
150 g (5½ oz) diced carrot
150 g (5½ oz) diced celery
100 ml (3½ fl oz) extra virgin olive oil
800 g (1 lb 12 oz) diced veal rump
salt and pepper, to taste
150 ml (5 fl oz) white wine
300 g (10½ oz) peeled tomatoes
1 rosemary sprig
400 g (14 oz) cooking cream

Ravioli filling
3 eggs
pinch of nutmeg
salt and pepper, to taste
50 g (1¾ oz) parmesan cheese

Crispy fried artichokes
2 artichokes, peeled and sliced
50 g (1¾ oz) plain (all-purpose) flour
250 ml (9 fl oz) soy/canola oil, for frying

pasta dough (see page 117)
50 g (1¾ oz) grated parmesan cheese, to serve

SERVES 6

In a pot over medium heat, sauté the diced vegetables with the olive oil. Add the diced veal, season with salt and pepper then lightly caramelize the meat. Add the wine and when it has evaporated, add the tomatoes and the rosemary. Cover the pot with a lid throughout the cooking time. Cook until the meat is tender. Add the cream and simmer for 10 minutes. Separate the meat and set the sauce aside.

Place the meat in a blender with the eggs, nutmeg, salt, pepper (to taste) and parmesan. Process until smooth. Set aside until needed.

To make the crispy fried artichokes, clean the artichokes, remove all the hard leaves until you reach the soft, pale yellow color. Cut the stalk close to the artichoke and finely slice the artichoke. Place the finely sliced artichoke in cold water. Squeeze the juice of 1 lemon and leave aside for 1 hour. Drain the artichokes, dust in flour and fry in soy or canola oil. Season with salt and pepper. Set aside until needed.

To make the pasta dough, add the flour to the bowl of a mixer on slow to medium speed and add the egg mixture to the flour. Mix until the flour and eggs are combined, and you have a smooth yellow dough. Add extra yolk if it appears a little dry. Take the dough out of the bowl and wrap with plastic wrap. Rest the dough for at least 1 hour, preferably in the fridge.

Use a pasta rolling machine to roll out the pasta. Clamp the pasta machine tightly to a table. Divide the

dough by 4 with a knife, keep the 4 pieces covered in plastic wrap to avoid drying out. Take one piece at a time and roll it through the machine repetitively by folding the dough at least 3–5 times until the dough is perfectly rectangular shape to the width of the machine. Start this at the highest setting. Repeat this passing the pasta through the machine on each setting until you reach setting 1. You will have a long thin pasta sheet.

Place a small ball (approximately 10 g/¼ oz) of the veal mixture, leaving approximately two finger spaces between each filling. Once you reach the end of the pasta sheet dividing the filling equally across, dip the brush in water and brush the opposite side of the filling. Fold the brushed side over the filling and push down in between each filling.

Using a ravioli cutter or knife, cut a square around each filling leaving approximately 2 cm (¾ in) around the filling. Once all the ravioli have been cut, press firmly down around the filling removing any air pockets. Repeat this with all the pasta dough until you have used all the filling.

Bring a pot of salted water to the boil. Blanch the ravioli and cook until they float to the top of the boiling water and ensure they are soft in the middle. Drain.

Meanwhile, in another pot, heat the remaining sauce saved from the veal mix. Add the ravioli and mix gently to coat.

Place the ravioli on a large flat plate and top with shaved parmesan and crispy fried artichokes.

Tip: With all the offcuts, do not dispose as you can use all of these for the Maltagliata Pasta recipe.

PASTA PISELLI E PANCETTA

Pasta with peas and pancetta

150 g (5½ oz) diced onion
150 g (5½ oz) prosciutto crudo
750 g (1 lb 10 oz) peas
1 garlic clove
1 l (35 fl oz) vegetable stock
500 g (1 lb 2 oz) tubetti pasta
flat-leaf (Italian) parsley, finely chopped, to garnish

SERVES 6

Heat the olive oil in a pot over medium heat. Add the garlic and sauté the diced onion and the prosciutto until the onion is translucent and the prosciutto is caramelized. Add the fresh peas and the vegetable stock and cook until the peas are soft and tender and have lost their bright green color.

Bring a pot of salted water to the boil. Add the pasta and cook for approximately half or less than recommended cooking time on the packet. Drain.

Add the pasta to the sauce and cook until all the vegetable stock has been absorbed and a creamy consistency has formed.

Tip: Retain some of the water from the pasta pot. You can use this to add to the sauce if required.

PASTA CON ZUCCA E SALSICCIA

Pasta with pumpkin and sausage

1 kg (2 lb 4 oz) diced pumpkin (winter squash)
100 g (3½ oz) extra virgin olive oil
5 garlic cloves
1 chilli, finely sliced
200 ml (7 fl oz) white wine
350 g (12 oz) sausage meat
50 g (1¾ oz) grated pecorino
salt and pepper, to taste
500 g (1 lb 2 oz) orecchiette pasta

SERVES 6

In a pot over medium heat, add the extra virgin olive oil, garlic and chilli. Add the sausage meat and cook until the meat is browned. Deglaze with the white wine. Cook the sausage through, then remove the sausage from the pot.

Add the diced pumpkin and reduce the heat to low. Simmer, covered, for approximately 20 minutes, or until the pumpkin is soft. Add the sausage and cook until the pasta is ready to be added.

Bring a pot of salted water to the boil. Add the pasta and cook for approximately 2 minutes less than recommended cooking time on the packet. Drain.

Add the pasta to the sauce and cook for approximately 2 minutes. Mix well and serve on a large plate and top with the grated pecorino.

RISOTTO CON CODA DI BUE E GREMOLATA

Ox tail risotto with gremolata

1 kg (2 lb 4 oz) ox tail
salt and pepper, to taste
100 ml (3½ fl oz) extra virgin olive oil
2 garlic cloves
125 g (4½ oz) diced celery
125 g (4½ oz) diced carrot
125 g (4½ oz) diced onion
175 g (6 oz) peeled tomatoes
75 g (2½ oz) tomato paste (concentrated purée)
500 ml (17 fl oz) red wine
500 ml (17 fl oz) vegetable stock
1 cinnamon stick
2 star anise
2 bay leaves
2 rosemary sprigs

Risotto
50 ml (1¾ fl oz) extra virgin olive oil
2 shallots
300 g (10½ oz) Carnaroli rice
150 ml (5 fl oz) white wine
1 l (35 fl oz) vegetable stock
50 g (1¾ oz) unsalted butter
50 g (1¾ oz) parmesan cheese

Orange gremolata recipe
30 g (1 oz) flat-leaf (Italian) parsley, finely chopped
2 garlic cloves
1 orange zest

SERVES 6

Lightly dust the ox tail in a salt and pepper flour mix. In a pan over medium heat, add the oil and seal each piece of the ox tail.

In a separate pan, add the oil and garlic and all the diced vegetables. Sauté then add the whole peeled tomatoes, tomato paste, red wine, cinnamon stick, star anise, bayleaf and rosemary. Add the vegetable stock and salt and pepper to taste.

Transfer the vegetable mixture onto a baking tray. Add the ox tail and cover with baking paper and foil. Place in the oven and allow to cook for 2 hours at 180°C (350°F) or until the meat falls off the bone.

To make the risotto, heat the extra virgin olive oil in a small pot. Sauté the diced shallots until they are transparent. Add the Carnaroli rice and cook over low heat. Once the rice is toasted, add the white wine and wait until wine is fully evaporated. Add a third of the vegetable stock and stir until absorbed then repeat until all vegetable stock has been used. Gently stir with a wooden spoon to avoid the rice from breaking. Add the butter and Parmigiano Reggiano. The risotto should have a creamy consistency.

Heat the ox tail. Portion the risotto into 6 equal potions and place the ox tail on top of the risotto. Garnish with the orange gremolata.

LASAGNA RAGÙ DI CARNE MISTA E BÉSCIAMELLA

Lasagna with mix meat ragu and bechamel sauce

Lasagne
600 g (1 lb 5 oz) fresh pasta sheets, homemade or from your favorite food store
100 g (3½ oz) butter
1 kg (2 lb 4 oz) ragù
250 g (9 oz) mozzarella cheese, roughly sliced
150 g (5½ oz) pecorino Romano cheese
20 basil leaves

Ragù
100 ml (3½ fl oz) olive oil
2 onion, finely diced
2 garlic cloves, finely chopped
100 g (3½ oz) pancetta, finely chopped
300 g (10½ oz) beef rump, cut into 3 cm (1¼ in) cubes
300 g (10½ oz) lamb leg, cut into 3 cm (1¼ in) cubes
300 g (10½ oz) pork shoulder, cut into 3 cm (1¼ in) cubes
250 g (9 oz) Italian fennel sausages
500 ml (17 fl oz) red wine
2 tablespoons tomato paste (concentrated purée)
2 bay leaves
1.5 l (52 fl oz) tomato passata (tomato purée)
10 basil leaves
salt and pepper, to taste

Béchamel sauce
750 g (1 lb 10 oz) béchamel
50 g (1¾ oz) unsalted butter
60 g (2¼ oz) plain (all-purpose) flour
750 ml (26 fl oz) milk
1 small onion, diced
6 black peppercorns
1 sprig fresh thyme
pinch of nutmeg
salt, to taste

SERVES 8

Recipe continues on page 73

To make the ragù, heat a large saucepan over high heat. Add the oil, onion, garlic, pancetta and cook until onions are soft. Add the beef, lamb, pork and sausages and season with salt and pepper. Cook the meats until browned. Add the red wine, cooking and stirring occasionally until all the wine is evaporated. Add the tomato paste and bay leaves and cook for a 2 minutes, stirring constantly. Add the passata turn to a low heat and simmer, slowly cooking the ragù until the meat is soft and tender, this will take a minimum of 2-3 hours then add basil and cook for a further 20 minutes and season to taste.

To make the béchamel sauce, warm the milk in a heavy-bottomed saucepan over medium heat, stirring occasionally. You just want it to be warm, about 45°C (113°F), not hot, and certainly not boiling.

Meanwhile, in a separate heavy-bottomed saucepan, melt the butter over medium heat. With a wooden spoon, stir the flour into the melted butter a little bit at a time, until it is fully incorporated into the butter, giving you a pale yellow colored paste called a roux. Heat the roux for another minute or so to cook off the taste of raw flour. Using a wire whisk, slowly add the warm milk to the roux, whisking vigorously to make sure it is free of lumps.

Now add the onion, peppercorn and thyme to the sauce. Simmer around 95°C (203 F) for about 20 minutes or until the total volume has reduced by about 20 percent, stirring frequently to make sure the sauce doesn't scorch at the bottom of the pan. The resulting sauce should be smooth and velvety. If it is too thick, whisk in a bit more milk until it is just thick enough to coat the back of a spoon. Remove the sauce from the heat. Remove the onion, peppercorn and thyme and discard. For an extra smooth consistency, carefully pour the sauce through a wire mesh strainer lined with a piece of cheesecloth. Season the sauce very lightly with salt and nutmeg.

Preheat the oven to 180°C (350°F). Grease a large baking dish (30 cm x 40 cm/12 in x 16 in) with butter and set aside.

Bring a large pot of salted water to the boil, and blanche the pasta sheets one at a time and cook until *al dente*. Refresh in a bowl of iced water (When all the pasta sheets are cooked and chilled, strain the water off and pat dry with a kitchen towels).

Spread a large spoonful of the ragù in the baking dish and place enough pasta sheets to cover the dish. Spread with the ragù, ¼ of the béchamel, ¼ of mozzarella, ¼ of pecorino Romano and 5 basil leaves. Repeat the process three more times or until all the pasta is finished. Add some ragù on top and bake for 30–40 minutes, or until golden crisp on top. Rest the lasagna for 10 minutes and then cut into portions to serve, garnished with grated pecorino and fresh basil leaves.

INVOLTINI DI MERLUZZO CON PINOLI E SEDANO

Rolls of whiting with pine nuts and celery

Crumb mixture
10 g (¼ oz) flat-leaf (Italian) parsley
4 g (⅛ oz) mint
1 garlic clove
½ chilli, chopped
1 lemon zest
20 g (¾ oz) pine nuts
50 g (1¾ oz) sultanas
10 g (¼ oz) breadcrumbs

Celery ach purée
1 kg (2 lb 4 oz) celery ach
10 g (¼ oz) salt
1 l (35 fl oz) water

12 x 70 g (2½ oz) whiting fillets
100 ml (3½ fl oz) Italian white wine
50 ml (1¾ fl oz) extra virgin olive oil
50 g (1¾ oz) zucchini (courgette)
50 g (1¾ oz) eggplant (aubergine)
50 g (1¾ oz) capsicum (pepper)
50 g (1¾ oz) celery
50 g (1¾ oz) red onion

SERVES 6

Preheat the oven to 200°C (400°F).

To make the crumb mixture, in a small bowl combine all the herbs, garlic, chilli, lemon zest, pine nuts, sultanas and breadcrumb.

Place the whiting flat on a chopping board, in line with no gaps between them. Layer the crumb mixture evenly across the whiting. Roll each fillet and skewer 2 fillets on each skewer.

Oil a baking tray and place each skewer in the tray. Sprinkle with salt and pepper. Bake for , 6–8 minutes or until the center is cooked.

To make the celery ach purée, dice the celery ach. Place in a pot with the water and cook until soft with the salt. All the water should be absorbed. Once cooked place in a blender, add the extra virgin olive oil and blitz to a smooth, creamy consistency.

Blanch the vegetables in boiling water rapidly, then quickly in salty water. Remove and refresh in ice water. Strain them from the ice water and pat dry and add extra virgin olive oil and mix well.

Spread the celery ach purée on a plate and place a skewer on top and sprinkle the vegetables over the whiting roughly.

Fish & Meat

INVOLTINI DI VITELLO

Veal rolls

40 g (1½ oz) flat-leaf (Italian) parsley
5 g (⅛ oz) garlic cloves
90 g (3¼ oz) pancetta

600 g (1 lb 5 oz) veal rump, 3 x 200 g (7 oz) each
250 g (9 oz) smoked buffalo mozzarella cheese
6 small to medium potatoes
3–4 artichokes
50 g (1¾ oz) extra virgin olive oil
salt and pepper, to taste
2 rosemary sprigs

SERVES 6

Preheat the oven to 200°C (400°F). Line a baking tray with baking paper.

Chop the parsley, garlic, pancetta salt and pepper all together until creating a smooth spread.

Butterfly the veal rump. Tenderise the veal. Cut the veal into 6 strips each approximately 6 cm (2½ in) each. Brush the parsley spreads on each piece of veal.

Cut the mozzarella into 18 pieces and layer on each piece of veal.

Roll each piece of veal and skewer 3 on each metal skewer.

Slice each potato 1 cm (¾ in) each, then cut and layer each potato separately on a baking tray lined.

Between each potato slice, add a slice of artichoke. Drizzle with extra virgin olive oil and salt and pepper.

Cover the tray with foil and place in the oven for 20 minutes, or until nice and soft.

Fish & Meat

POLLO CON CARCIOFI E PISELLI

Chicken with artichokes and peas

80 ml (2½ fl oz) olive oil
1 whole chicken, cut into quarters
2 garlic cloves, minced
½ cup chopped flat-leaf (Italian) parsley
1 tablespoon chopped marjoram
125 ml (4 fl oz) white wine
fresh artichoke (outer leaves removed and cut into halves), cut into 8 pieces
100 g (3½ oz) peas
250 ml (9 fl oz) chicken stock
salt and pepper, to taste

SERVES 4

Heat the oil in a heavy-based saucepan over medium–high heat. Add the chicken, season and cook until browned.

Add the garlic, parsley and marjoram and gently fry for 2–3 minutes. Add the wine and cook out the alcohol.

Add the chicken stock along with the artichoke and peas, cover with a lid and cook on a low heat for 40 minutes, or until tender.

CAPRETTO ALLA PIZZAIOLA

Baby Goat Pizzaiola

2 kg (4 lb 8 oz) goat shoulder, diced
1 onion, peeled and diced
3 garlic cloves
½ cup chopped flat-leaf (Italian) parsley
2 tablespoons dried oregano
100 ml (3½ fl oz) olive oil
bay leaves
2.4 kg (5 lb 8 oz) very ripe cherry tomatoes
100 ml (3½ fl oz) white wine
30 g (1 oz) capers
100 g (3½ oz) black olives
40 g (1½ oz) grated pecorino cheese
50 g (1¾ oz) breadcrumbs
salt and pepper, to taste

SERVES 10

Preheat the oven to 210°C (415°F).

Season the goat shoulder with salt and pepper. Place in a heavy baking dish and add the onions and garlic. Sprinkle over the parsley, oregano, olive oil and bay leaves.

Crush the cherry tomatoes with your hand and spread them over the top. Add the wine.

Roast for 1½ hours, then add the capers, black olives, pecorino cheese and breadcrumbs. Roast for a further 5 minutes (enough to brown the pecorino and breadcrumbs). You should be able to poke a fork into the meat easily. Serve immediately.

COSTOLETTE DI AGNELLO CON PISELLI, FAVE E PANCETTA

Lamb ribs on peas, broad beans and pancetta

Lamb
6 lamb ribs
3 garlic cloves, chopped
1 chilli, chopped
120 ml (4 fl oz) extra virgin olive oil
45 ml (1½ fl oz) balsamic vinegar
zest and juice of 1 lemon
4.5 g (⅛ oz) thyme, chopped
35 g (1¼ oz) rosemary, chopped
salt and pepper, to taste

500 g (1 lb 2 oz) baby peas
500 g (1 lb 2 oz) peeled broad beans
60 g (2¼ oz) diced shallots
60 g (2¼ oz) diced pancetta
½ garlic clove, minced
20 g (¾ oz) chopped mint
60 ml (2 fl oz) extra virgin olive oil
vegetable stock (enough to cover)

Salsa verde
1 large anchovy
5 capers, rinsed
10 basil leaves
½ bunch chervil
1 bunch chives, chopped
20 flat-leaf (Itlaian) parsley leaves
15 ml (½ fl oz) white wine vinegar
85 ml (2¾ fl oz) extra virgin olive oil
juice of ½ lemon
1 garlic clove
salt, to taste

SERVES 6

Preheat the oven to 82°C (180°F). To prepare the lamb, trim a bit of fat off the lamb between the skin and ribs. Combine all of the ingredients and marinate the lamb ribs. Place both ribs together in oven heat bags and place in the oven to steam for minimum of 8 hours.

To make the pea mixture, sauté the shallots, garlic, pancetta and olive oil in a pot over medium heat until soft and the pancetta is crispy. Add the baby peas and broad beans. Add the vegetable stock to cover. Cook slowly for at least 1 hour, or until the peas are soft and mushy. Add mint close to end, then season.

To make the salsa verde, place the shallots, anchovy, capers, bread, vinegar and chopped parsley in a blender. Process until smooth. Place the purée in a bowl, then add the chopped tarragon, chervil, chives and fold together. Add the olive oil and season with salt.

In a hot bath water, warm up the bag with the lamb inside for approximately 20 minutes. Carefully remove the bag. Open the bag and place lamb on a tray lined with baking paper.

Preheat the oven to 200°C (400°F). Remove from the oven when the ribs are nicely crisp. With skin down divide the rack by three and place on a bed of beans. Garnish with salsa verde and fresh herbs.

Fish & Meat

CONIGLIO ALL'ISCHITANA

Ischitana rabbit

1 rabbit
250 ml (9 fl oz) white wine
1 rosemary sprig, chopped
½ bunch basil
oregano, to taste
13 peeled tomatoes
125 ml (4 fl oz) extra virgin olive oil

SERVES 4

Wash the rabbit well, then cut into serving portions and allow to dry.

Heat the extra virgin olive oil in a heavy casserole pot. Add the rabbit to the pot and cook over very low heat.

Once the juices from the rabbit have evaporated, add the wine, salt, pepper and peeled tomato. Add the rosemary and basil with 750 ml (26 fl oz) of water.

Cover with a lid and cook for 2 hours.

Fish & Meat

AGNELLO AL FORNO CON PATATE

Roasted lamb with potatoes

1.8 kg (4 lb) lamb shoulder, diced into pieces
3 onions, peeled and cut into quarters
3 garlic cloves
20 g (¾ oz) flat-leaf (Italian) parsley, chopped
2 tablespoons dried oregano
2 kg (4 lb 8 oz) very ripe cherry tomatoes
100 ml (3½ fl oz) olive oil
1 kg (2 lb 4 oz) peeled potatoes, cut into quarters
100 ml (3½ fl oz) white wine
3 bay leaves
1 tablespoon rosemary
salt and pepper, to taste

SERVES 8

Preheat the oven to 210°C (415°F).

Season the lamb salt and pepper and place in a heavy baking dish. Add the onions, potatoes and garlic. Sprinkle over the parsley, oregano, olive oil, rosemary and bay leaves.

Crush the cherry tomatoes with your hand and spread them over the top. Add the wine and roast for 1½ hours. You should be able to poke a fork into the meat easily. Serve immediately.

BRACIOLE RIPIENI CON MOZZARELA E FRIARELLI

Chops stuffed with mozzarella and friarelli

150 g (5½ oz) friarelle (Neapolitan broccoli), chopped
100 g (3½ oz) mozzarella, diced
50 g (1¾ oz) toasted pine nuts
50 g (1¾ oz) sultanas
25 g (1 oz) grated parmesan cheese
6 slices of beef muscle (ask your butcher for this), about 150 g (5½ oz) each
100 ml (3½ fl oz) olive oil
3 garlic cloves, minced
1 large onion, peeled and chopped
125 ml (4 fl oz) dry white wine
1 kg (2 lb 4 oz) peeled tomatoes
salt and pepper to taste, to taste

SERVES 6

Combine the friarelle, mozzarella, pine nuts, sultanas and parmesan in a bowl.

Lay out the beef slices on a flat surface. Add a large tablespoon of the friarelle mixture on each slice. Roll up the braciole and tightly tie with string.

In a heavy-based pot, add the olive oil, garlic, onion and lightly fry over medium heat. Add the braciole and season with salt and pepper. Fry the braciole over high heat until golden brown.

Add the white wine and cook out the alcohol. Add the peeled tomatoes and bring to the boil. Cover with a lid and cook for 1½ hours, or until the braciole are tender.

Remove the braciole from the sauce and carefully undo the string. Slice into 2 cm (¾ in) rounds and arrange on the plate, spooning the sauce over the top.

QUAGLIE CON PATATE

Quails with potatoes

4 quails
250 ml (9 fl oz) extra virgin olive oil
1 onion, diced
3 potatoes, quartered
13 peeled tomatoes
250 ml (9 fl oz) white wine
1 handful basil
salt and pepper, to taste
peperoncino (fresh chilli optional), to taste

SERVES 2

Heat the oil in a pan over medium heat. Add the onion and simmer until transparent.

Add the quail and cook on one side for 3–5 minutes, then turn over. Add the white wine and pepper to taste.

Add the potato, cover with a lid and cook for 3-5 minutes. Add the tomato evenly over the quails, then add basil. Cook for about 10 minutes, then add salt to taste.

Continue to cook for approximately 25–30 minutes.

Fish & Meat

GIRELLO

Slow cooked silverside

250 ml (9 fl oz) extra virgin olive oil
6 large onions, diced
1 handful flat-leaf (Italian) parsley, chopped
cracked pepper, to taste
2 kg (4 lb 8 oz) girello
250 ml (9 fl oz) white wine

SERVES 10

Add the oil, onion, parsley and pepper to a pot over medium heat. Cook until the onion has colored. Stir the onions frequently to avoid burning.

Add the girello to the pot and allow to simmer on one side, approximately 4–5 minutes, then turn the girello over. Repeat 3–4 times again, ensuring the onions do not burn.

Add the white wine. After 15 minutes of searing, add 2 liters (70 fl oz) of water, or enough to cover the girello. Allow to cook for 4 hours. Once cooked, allow to rest for 1 day.

Cut the girello into slices. Add to a pan with the onion sauce and heat. When serving, add the onion sauce over the sliced girello.

DOLCI

5

Desserts

BABA' CON CREMA PASTICCERA

Rum baba with custard

Baba
50 g (1¾ oz) yeast
250 ml (9 fl oz) milk
1 kg (2 lb 4 oz) flour, sifted
150 g (5½ oz) castor sugar
400 g (14 oz) unsalted butter
4 eggs, lightly beaten
3 egg yolks, lightly beaten
zest of 1 orange and 1 lemon

Syrup for baba
1 l (35 fl oz) water
500 g (1 lb 2 oz) castor sugar
rum extract, to taste
zest of 1 lemon

Crème patissier
8 egg yolks
185 g (6½ oz) castor sugar
135 g (4¾ oz) plain (all-purpose) flour
1,100 ml (37 fl oz) milk
2 vanilla pods

SERVES 6

Dissolve the yeast in some warm milk until it becomes frothy.

Put the flour and sugar in a bowl and make a well in the center. Add the yeast mixture to form a soft, sticky dough. Add a little more milk if the mix is too dry. Shape into a ball and knead until smooth. Place in a bowl and leave in a warm place to rise to double in size.

When it has doubled in size, remove and incorporate the remaining ingredients, kneading well to ensure it is mixed and becomes smooth and elastic.

Pour the dough into a lightly greased and floured baba mould. Cover with plastic wrap, leave in a warm place and allow to rise to the top of the mould.

Bake at 180°C (350°F) for 20 minutes, or until golden and cooked through when tested with a skewer. While cooking keep the oven door closed at all times until ready to test with skewer.

Meanwhile, make the syrup for the baba. Place the water, sugar, lemon zest and a few drops of the rum extract in a pot and bring to the boil until the sugar has dissolved. Remove from the heat and allow the syrup to cool.

When the baba are cooked and still warm, pour the cooled syrup over the baba. Before serving, add a splash of rum if desired.

To make the crème patissier, place the egg yolks into a bowl. Add the sugar and mix together. Sift the flour and add to the egg mixture. Place milk and vanilla pods into a pot and bring to the boil. Remove the vanilla pods and pour over the egg mixture slowly while whisking. Place the mixture into a clean pot and heat again to cook out the starch in the flour. Allow to cool.

Once your pastry crème is cooked, fill the baba.

—Desserts—

PASTIERA NAPOLETANA

Pastiera Napoletana

Sweet Pastry
100 g (3½ oz) castor sugar
200 g (7 oz) unsalted butter
1 egg
300 g (10½ oz) plain (all-purpose) flour

Pastiera
300 ml (10½ fl oz) milk
500 g (1 lb 2 oz) grano cotto (cooked wheat)
1 tablespoon unsalted butter
700 g (1 lb 9 oz) ricotta cheese
200 g (7 oz) castor sugar
7 eggs
3 egg yolks
10 ml (¼ fl oz) vanilla extract
370 g (13 oz) candied orange peel, finely chopped

SERVES 8

Preheat the oven to 160°C (315°F).

Cream the butter and sugar using an electric mixer on low speed. Once the butter and sugar are combined, add the egg and the flour. Mix until all the ingredients are combined, but don't overmix. Roll the sweet pastry over a tart tin 25–30 cm wide x 15 cm high (10–12 in x 6 in). Reserve the pastry offcuts for the top of the tart.

To make the pastiera, place the milk and grano cotto in a pot over medium heat and cook for 10 minutes. Add the butter and stir until melted. Remove from the heat and set aside to cool. Mix the ricotta and sugar using electric beaters for 5 minutes. Add the eggs and egg yolks and mix well. Add a few drops of the vanilla extract and mix well. Pour the mixture into the sweet pastry case.

Using the leftover sweet pastry, cut 2 cm (¾ in) strips the length of your tart case. Place 2 strips approximately 4 cm (1½ in) apart in one direction, then repeat crossing in the opposite direction.

Bake for 15 minutes, or until lightly golden. You can eat the pastiera without any sides, alternatively you can add some cream or gelato.

TORTA CAPRESE

Caprese Cake

3 eggs, separated
200 g (7 oz) sugar
250 g (9 oz) unsalted butter
250 g (9 oz) cooking chocolate
250 g (9 oz) hazelnut flour

Chocolate sauce
1 l (35 fl oz) cream
800 g (1 lb 12 oz) cooking chocolate
orange extract

SERVES 8

Preheat the oven to 160°C (315°F). Lightly grease a 23 cm (9 in) round spring form cake tin.

Whip the egg yolks in a bowl with half the sugar.

In a separate bowl, whip the egg whites with the remaining sugar until stiff.

Melt the chocolate and the butter together in a bowl placed over a pot of simmering water. Once the chocolate and butter has melted, remove from the heat and add the hazelnut flour, folding to combine.

Fold the yolk mix through the chocolate, followed by the egg white mixture.

Pour the mixture into the tin and bake for 20–25 minutes.

To make the chocolate sauce, place the cream, chocolate and a few drops of the orange extract in a pot and cook, stirring over a low heat. Allow the chocolate to melt, stirring frequently. Once all the chocolate has melted, remove from the heat.

Pour the chocolate sauce over the cake. Serve warm.

BIGNE CON CREMA AL CIOCCOLATO

Beignets with chocolate cream

250 ml (9 fl oz) water
100 g (3½ oz) unsalted butter
250 ml (9 fl oz) plain (all-purpose) flour
¼ teaspoon salt
4 eggs

Crème patissier
2 egg yolks
45 g (1½ oz) castor sugar
35 g (1¼ oz) plain (all-purpose) flour
275 ml (9¼ fl oz) milk
½ vanilla pod

Chocolate
60 ml (2 fl oz) milk
50 g (1¾ oz) dark chocolate
125 ml (4¼ fl oz) cream

SERVES 12

Preheat the oven to 220°C (425°F).

In a large pot, bring the water and butter to a rolling boil. Stir in the flour and salt until the mixture forms a ball. Transfer the dough to a large mixing bowl.

Using a wooden spoon or stand mixer, beat in the eggs one at a time, mixing well after each addition. Drop use a piping bag or drop tablespoons of the mix onto an ungreased baking tray.

Bake for 20–25 minutes, or until golden brown. The centers should be dry.

When the shells are cool, either split and fill them with the crème patissier mixture, or use a pastry bag to pipe the filling into the shells.

To make the crème patissier, place the egg yolks into a bowl. Add the sugar and mix together. Sift the flour and add to the egg mixture. Place milk and vanilla pods into a pot and bring to the boil. Remove the vanilla pods and pour over the egg mixture slowly while whisking. In another pot prepare the chocolate mix, add milk, dark chocolate and the cream and allow all to combine. Place the other mixture into a clean pot and heat again to cook out the starch in the flour. While cooking add the chocolate mixture slowly into the pot and whisk.

Allow to cool, cover and then refrigerate. Use the mixture to fill the bigne.

PANNACOTTA AL MIELE

Pannacotta with honey

2 gelatin sheets
300 ml (10 fl oz) cream
100 ml (3⅖ fl oz) milk
16 g (½ oz) castor sugar
80 g (2¾ oz) honey

SERVES 6

Soak the gelatin in a bowl of cold water.

Place the cream and milk into a pot over low heat. Gently heat but make sure it does not get to boiling point or at a simmer.

Add the honey and sugar. Once the temperature reaches 60–70°C (140–150°F) add the gelatin and stir. Remove from the heat.

Spray the panna cotta moulds and pour the mixture into the moulds. Leave to set in the fridge, covered.

TORTINO AL CIOCCOLATO

Chocolate fondant

85 g (3 oz) unsalted butter
135 g (4¾ oz) dark chocolate
45 g (1½ oz) unsweetened cocoa powder
45 g (1½ oz) cornflour (cornstarch)
1 g (³⁄₁₀ oz) baking powder
145 g (1 lb 12 oz) plain (all-purpose) flour
5 whole eggs
200 g (7 oz) castor sugar

SERVES 6

Preheat the oven to 200°C (400°F). Lightly grease six 100 ml capacity ramekins.

Place the butter and dark chocolate in a bowl and set over a bowl of hot water. Stir until melted.

Sift all of dry ingredients in a bowl.

Whisk the eggs and sugar together in a separate bowl. Slowly pour the chocolate mixture into the egg mixture, whisking to combine.

Fold the dry ingredients into the chocolate mixture. Spoon the mixture into the ramekins.

Bake for 6–7 minutes, or until the outside is cooked. Test this by inserting a thin wooden skewer into the edge of the pudding, if it comes out clean then it is cooked. You want the heart of the pudding to remain runny. Remove from the oven and allow to cool slightly. Remove the puddings gently and turn upside down.

Serve warm with a side of vanilla gelato.

6

INSALATA

Salad

INSALATA DI BARBABIETOLE

Beetroot salad

300 g (10½ oz) beetroot
300 g (10½ oz) golden beetroot
60 g (2¼ oz) rocket (arugula) leaves
90 g (3¼ oz) goat's cheese
120 g (4¼ oz) caramelised walnuts (see page 129)
30 g (1 oz) salad dressing (see page 129)

SERVES 6

Preheat the oven to 180°C (350°F).

Cover each beetroot with foil and place on a baking tray. Roast for approximately 40–45 minutes, or until a metal skewer passes through the beetroot. Allow to cool.

Once the beetroot has cooled, peel and cut into the desired size. Season with salt and pepper.

Arrange the beetroots on plate, sprinkle the rocket leaves on top, then add the goat's cheese and candied walnuts. Drizzle with the salad dressing. Serve immediately.

INSALATA DI FINOCCHIO E ARANCIA

Fennel & orange salad

270 g (9½ oz) washed radicchio
240 g (8½ oz) thinly sliced fennel
300 g (10½ oz) orange, sliced into 6 cm (2½ in) pieces, thick skin and pith removed
60 ml (2 fl oz) olive oil
20 ml (¾ fl oz) red wine vinegar
10 g (¼ oz) salt flakes
cracked pepper, to taste
20 g (¾ oz) salted ricotta, finely grated

SERVES 6

Add the radicchio, fennel and orange to a large bowl. Add the oil, vinegar and salt and pepper and gently toss to combine.

Top with the ricotta and serve immediately.

INSALATA DI RUCOLA

Rocket salad

210 g (7½ oz) rocket (arugula) leaves
150 g (5½ oz) sliced pears
30 g (1 oz) balsamic dressing
135 g (4¾ oz) raspadura cheese, shaved
rocket salad dressing (page 129), to taste
balsamic reduction, to taste

SERVES 6

Add the rocket leaves, sliced pears, raspadura cheese and rocket salad dressing to a large bowl and toss gently to combine.

Arrange the salad on a serving plate and drizzle with the balsamic reduction.

INSALATA CAPRESE

Caprese salad

400 g (14 oz) buffalo mozzarella cheese, sliced
420 g (15 oz) heirloom tomatoes, sliced
9 g (¼ oz) basil leaves
30 ml (1 fl oz) extra virgin olive oil
salt and pepper, to taste

SERVES 6

Place the tomato and the mozzarella on a serving plate, alternating overlapping each other.

Add the basil leaves in between the tomato and mozzarella. Season with salt and pepper and drizzle with the extra virgin olive oil.

Serve at room temperature.

IL CAPITOLO FONDAMENTALE

Basics

RICETTA DI PASTA FRESCA

Fresh pasta recipe

1 kg (2 lb 4 oz) le 5 stagioni 00 pasta flour
2 eggs
up to 600 ml (21 fl oz) egg yolks, including 2 whole eggs

MAKES 16 SERVES AT 100G PORTIONS

To make the pasta dough, add the flour to the bowl of a mixer. Set the speed to slow to medium and add the egg to the flour. Mix until the flour and eggs are combined and you have a smooth yellow dough. Add extra yolk if it appears a little dry.

Remove the dough from of the bowl and wrap with plastic wrap. Rest the dough for at least 1 hour, preferably in the fridge.

The best method to roll the pasta is using a pasta rolling machine. Clamp the pasta machine tightly to a table. Divide the dough into four equal portions with a knife. Keep the portions covered in plastic wrap to avoid drying out.

Take one piece at a time and roll it through the machine repetitively by folding the dough at least 3–5 times until the dough is perfectly rectangular shape to the width of the machine. Start this at the highest setting. Repeat passing the pasta through the machine on each setting until you reach setting 1. You will have a long thin pasta sheet.

Wrap in cling wrap and regrigerate. Store up to 2 days.

RAVIOLI

Ravioli

Use the fresh pasta recipe.

MAKES APPROXIMATLEY 16 SERVES

Use a pasta rolling machine to roll out the pasta. Clamp the pasta machine tightly to a table. Divide the dough into 4 with a knife, keep the 4 pieces covered in plastic wrap to avoid drying out. Take one piece at a time and roll it through the machine repetitively by folding the dough at least 3–5 times until the dough is perfectly rectangular shape to the width of the machine. Start this at the highest setting. Repeat this passing the pasta through the machine on each setting until you reach setting 1. You will have a long thin pasta sheet.

Place a small ball (approximately 10 g/¼ oz) of the mixture, leaving approximately two finger spaces between each filling. Once you reach the end of the pasta sheet dividing the filling equally across, dip the brush in water and brush the opposite side of the filling. Fold the brushed side over the filling and push down in between each filling.

Using a ravioli cutter or knife, cut a square around each filling leaving approximately 2 cm (¾ in) around the filling. Once all the ravioli have been cut, press firmly down around the filling removing any air pockets. Repeat this with all the pasta dough until you have used all the filling.

Repeat this with all the pasta dough until you have used all the filling. (Keep any pasta off-cuts as you can use all of these for the Matagliati pasta recipe. See page 49.)

SALSA ROSÈ

Rose sauce

50 g (3¾ oz) unsalted butter
1 onion, diced
½ tablespoon dried chilli, or to taste
750 ml (25½ fl oz) tomato paste (concentrated purée)
625 ml (21 fl oz) cream
625 ml (21 fl oz) chicken stock
salt, to taste

MAKES APPROX. ENOUGH FOR 20 ARANCINI BALLS

In a pot over medium heat, sauté the butter, onion and chilli until soft. Add the tomato paste and cook over low heat for approximately 10 minutes, stirring constantly.

Add the cream and chicken stock and cook for at least 30 minutes over low heat, stirring constantly. It will pop like lava so be careful and cover if required.

Remove from the heat, then blend the mixture until you have a smooth consistency.

Store in a sealed container and refrigerate up to 3 days.

RAGÙ DI FUNGHI

Mushroom ragu

130 ml (4½ fl oz) olive oil
200 g (7 oz) diced onion
15 g (½ fl oz) minced garlic
pinch of chopped thyme
pinch of chopped rosemary
1 kg (2 lb 4 oz) portobello mushrooms
350 g (12 oz) shiitake mushrooms
600 g (1 lb 5 oz) oyster mushrooms
15 g (½ fl oz) salt

MAKES APPROXIMATELY 1KG (2 LB 4 OZ) OF RAGU

Heat the oil in a large heavy-based pot over medium heat. Add the onion, garlic, thyme, rosemary and portobello mushrooms and sauté until soft. Add the shiitake mushrooms and sauté until soft. Add the oyster mushrooms.

Add the salt and cook until all the moisture has evaporated and the mushrooms resemble a ragù.

Store in a sealed container and refrigerate up to 3 days.

Tip: Use the sauce with any pasta you like. Add some cream to the ragu when cooking your pasta or simply leave it how it is. Or use the ragu in the Lasagna, either with the Napoli sauce or just with the béchamel.

SALSA ALLA NAPOLETANA

Napoli sauce

60 ml (2 fl oz) extra virgin olive oil
1 garlic clove, crushed
½ brown onion, diced
10 basil leaves, chopped
2.8 kg (6 lb) peeled tomato
20 g (¾ oz) salt
pinch of cracked pepper

MAKES APPROX. 2 L

Heat the olive oil in a large pot over medium heat. Add the garlic and lightly brown, then add the chopped brown onions and 5 basil leaves. Cook until the onions are golden brown.

Add the tomatoes and increase the heat to high. Keep stirring and bring to the boil. Once the sauce is boiling, reduce the flame to low and simmer for 45 minutes. Continue stirring every 5 minutes.

Season with salt and pepper and the remaining basil. Stir well and remove from the heat.

Store in a sealed container and refrigerate up to 3 days.

Tip: Use the sauce to cook with any pasta you like. Substitute the meat sauce in the lasagna and turn your meat lasagne into a vegetarian lasagna.

GNOCCHI

Gnocchi

1 kg (2 lb 4 oz) Dutch cream potatoes, mashed
pinch of nutmeg powder
1 egg
1 teaspoon salt
330 g (11½ oz) 5 stagioni pasta fresca flour

MAKES 6—8 SERVES

Place the potatoes in a pan of cold water and bring to the boil. Cook for 15 minutes, or until tender. Allow the potatoes to cool slightly, then peel.

Pass the potatoes through a potato masher into a large bowl. Turn the mash potato out onto a bench. Make a well in the center and add the nutmeg, eggs and salt. Sift in the flour, a little at a time. Using your hands, gently mix to a soft dough, adding a little extra flour if too sticky (don't overwork or gnocchi will be tough).

Cut a handful of dough and roll into a long 2 cm (¾ in) log. Using a spatula, cut the strip into 2 cm (¾ in) gnocchi. Place onto a lightly floured tray, then repeat with remaining dough. At this stage, you can set the gnocchi aside, covered with a tea towel, for 2–3 hours until ready to cook.

Cook the gnocchi, in two batches, in a large pan of boiling salted water. As soon as they rise to the surface (30–60 seconds), remove to a tray using a slotted spoon.

After fresh cooked, store for up to 3 days in a sealed container. Add a little olive oil to avoid sticking.

-Basics-

CONDIMENTO CON SALSA AL LIMONE

Lemon dressing for carpaccio

60 ml (2 fl oz) extra virgin olive oil
6 ml (¼ fl oz) freshly squeezed lemon juice
salt, to taste

MAKES 6 SERVES

Combine all of the ingredients in a jar and shake well.

Refrigerate and keep up to 3 days.

CONDIMENTO CON SALSA ALL'AGLIO E LIMONE

Lemon garlic dressing

25 ml (1 fl oz) lemon juice
25 ml (1 fl oz) sherry vinegar
1 garlic clove, minced
3 ml (1/10 oz) dijon mustard
200 ml (6¾ fl oz) blended olive oil
thyme, to taste
salt, to taste

MAKES 6 SERVES

Place the lemon juice, sherry vinegar, garlic, dijon and thyme leaves in a large bowl. Slowly add the oil using a stick blender to emulsify. Season to taste.

Put all the ingredients in a jar and shake well.

Refrigerate and keep up to 3 days.

CONDIMENTO DELL'INSALATA DI BARBABIETOLA

Beetroot salad dressing

100 ml (3½ fl oz) extra virgin olive oil
10 ml (¼ fl oz) sherry vinegar
10 ml (¼ fl oz) red wine vinegar
1 teaspoon lemon juice
2.5 ml (¹⁄₁₀ oz) dijon mustard
½ garlic cloves, grated
salt and pepper, to taste

MAKES 6

Place all of the ingredients in a large mixing bowl and mix with a stick blender. Add salt and pepper to taste.

Put all the ingredients in a jar and shake well.

Refrigerate and keep up to 3 days.

NOCI CARAMMELLATE

Caramelised walnuts

100 ml (3½ fl oz) water
100 g (3½ oz) brown sugar
100 g (3½ oz) walnuts

SERVES 6

Place the walnuts in a bowl of water and set aside for 30 minutes. Drain them, then dry on a rack for 2 hours.

Bring the water and sugar to the boil in a saucepan over medium heat. Add the walnuts to the pan, constantly mix the walnuts through the syrup until golden and caramelised. Season with salt and leave to cool.

Store in a sealed container and dry. Store for up to 3 days.

AÏOLI DI PEPERONI ROSSI È MANDORLE

Red capsicum & almond aïoli

500 g (1 lb 2 oz) red capsicum (pepper) (to make 375 g (13 oz) roasted strained capsicum purée)
50 g (1¾ oz) toasted almond meal
500 ml (17 fl oz) garlic aïoli (see page 133)
pinch of salt

SERVES 10

Roast the capsicum over a chargrill or bake in an oven until blackened. Place in a bowl and cover with plastic wrap for 30 minutes. When cooled, peel and the skin and remove the seeds. Purée in a food processor and drain for 2 hours.

Toast the almond meal in the oven at 140°C (275°F) for 40 minutes, turning constantly. Remove from the oven and set aside to cool.

Combine all of the ingredients in a blender or food processor and blend until smooth.

Put all the ingredients in a sealed jar. Refrigerate and keep up to 3 days.

AÏOLI
Garlic aïoli

2 whole eggs
3 egg yolks
15 ml (½ fl oz) white wine vinegar
2.5 ml (⅒ oz) mustard
6 garlic cloves
1 l (35 fl oz) vegetable oil
lemon juice, to taste
salt, to taste

SERVES 10

Place the whole eggs, yolks, vinegar, mustard and garlic in large bowl. Slowly add the oil and blend using a stick blender to emulsify.

Add the lemon juice and salt to taste.

Put all the ingredients in a sealed jar. Refrigerate and keep up to 3 days.

Tip: With left over aioli, you can use as a dipping sauce for fries, calamari or what ever else you may want to dip.

Or simply use the remainder for the Capsicum and Almond Aioli (See page 132).

BRODO VEGETALE
Vegetable stock

200 g (7 oz) onions
120 g (4¼ oz) carrots
150 g (5¼ oz) celery
5 g (²⁄₁₀ oz) peppercorns
1 bayleaf
3 g (⅒ oz) vegetable oil
3 l (101½ fl oz) water

MAKES APPROX. 2.25 L

In a large pot add the onion, carrots, celery, peppercorns and bay leaves, 3 liters (101.44 fl oz) of cold water and oil. Bring the stock to the boil, then simmer for 45 minutes.

Strain (remove as much of the vegetables first if that makes it easier), cool and refrigerate up to 3 days.

Portion in small containers. You can choose to freeze so you have stock on had at all times.

BRODO DI PESCE
Fish stock

20 ml (¾ fl oz) vegetable oil
5 kg (11 lb) white fish bones (using a knife, hit the bones creating a small cut)
2 small carrots, roughly chopped
⅓ bunch celery, roughly chopped
1 bulb fennel, roughly chopped
3 onions, roughly chopped
10 g (¼ oz) peppercorns
2 bay leaves

MAKES 8 L

Heat the oil in a large pot over medium heat. Add the fish bones and vegetables and cook for 10 minutes.

Add the peppercorns and bay leaves and 10 liters (338 fl oz) of cold water. Bring the stock to the boil, then simmer for 2 hours.

Strain (remove fish bones first if that makes it easier), cool and refrigerate up to 3 days.

Portion in small containers. You can choose to freeze so you have stock on had at all times.

BISQUE DI ASTICE
Bisque

1 onion
½ carrot
¼ celery stick
1 crayfish head
5 l (169 fl oz) fish stock (see previous recipe)
2 bay leaves
2–3 black peppercorns
200 g (7 oz) tomato paste (concentrated purée)

SERVES 4—6

Preheat the oven to 220°C (425°F).

Place all the vegetables and crayfish in a roasting tray. Roast in the oven for 15–18 minutes.

Crush the crayfish head with a hammer.

Place the vegetables and crayfish and fish stock in a stock pot over medium heat. Add the bay leaves, peppercorns and tomato paste. Bring to the boil, then reduce the flame to low.

Cook for 3–4 hours, or until bisque is thick like sauce. During the cooking process, skim the foam from the surface throughout the cooking time.

Once bisque is ready, strain it twice. Firstly using big sieve and then strained through a fine sieve.

FIORI DI ZUCCA IN PASTELLA

Zucchini flower batter

125 ml (4 fl oz) plain (all-purpose) flour
125 ml (4 fl oz) rice flour
270 ml (9½ fl oz) soda water
salt

MAKES 6

Combine all of the ingredients in a large bowl and whisk. Refrigerate until needed.

Basics

Index

A
Arancini   16

B
Baby Goat Pizzaiola   81
Beef carpaccio   25
Beetroot salad   107
Beetroot salad dressing   129
Beignets with chocolate cream   99
Bisque   135
Bocconcini   17

C
Caponata   33
Caprese Cake   97
Caprese salad   113
Chicken with artichokes and peas   80
Chocolate fondant   103
Chops stuffed with mozzarella and friarelli   87
Crab ravioli with mascarpone and sour tomato sauce   59

D
Drowned baby octopus   29

E
Eggplant in oil   44
Eggplant parmigiana   22

F
Fennel & orange salad   108
Fish stock   135
Fresh pasta recipe   117

G
Garlic aioli   133
Gnocchi   124

I
Ischitana rabbit   84

L
Lamb ribs on peas, broad beans and pancetta   83
Lasagna with mix meat ragu and bechamel sauce   70
Lemon dressing for carpaccio   128
Lemon garlic dressing   128
Linguine with zucchini flowers, zucchini and clams   56

M
Maltagliati with mussels and capsicum   49
Meatballs   15
Mushroom ragu   121

N
Napoli sauce   123

O

Ox tail risotto with gremolata   69

P

Paccherri with Genovese octopus   50
Pannacotta with honey   100
Pasta mixed with cauliflower, anchovies and pine nuts   53
Pasta with beans and mussels   52
Pasta with peas and pancetta   65
Pasta with pumpkin and sausage   66
Pastiera Napoletana   96
Pickled vegetables in oil   45

Q

Quails with potatoes   89

R

Ravioli   118
Red capsicum & almond aioli   132
Roasted lamb with potatoes   86
Rocket salad   112
Rolls of whiting with pine nuts and celery   77
Rose sauce   120
Rum baba with custard   95

S

Salt cod fritters   30

Sardines in oil   40
Seafood risotto   60
Seafood salad   34
Slow cooked silverside   90
Stuffed mushrooms   18
Stuffed mussels   26

T

Tuna in oil   39

V

Veal ravioli with artichoke sauce   62
Veal rolls   78
Vegetable stock   133

Z

Zucchini flower batter   136
Zucchini flowers with crab filling   21

First published in 2017 by New Holland Publishers
London • Sydney • Auckland

The Chandlery 50 Westminster Bridge Road London SE1 7QY United Kingdom
1/66 Gibbes Street Chatswood NSW 2067 Australia
5/39 Woodside Ave Northcote Auckland 0627 New Zealand

www.newhollandpublishers.com

Copyright © 2017 New Holland Publishers
Copyright © 2017 in text: Johnny Di Francesco
Copyright © 2017 in images: New Holland Publishers, Shutterstock: page 6, 32, 48, 54, 55, 63, 74–75, 92–93, 122, 130–131, 138–139, 142 and 143.

All rights reserved. No part of this publication may be reproduced, stored in a retrieval system or transmitted, in any form or by any means, electronic, mechanical, photocopying, recording or otherwise, without the prior written permission of the publishers and copyright holders.

A record of this book is held at the British Library and the National Library of Australia.

ISBN: 9781742577296

Group Managing Director: Fiona Schultz
Publisher: Monique Butterworth
Project Editor: Gordana Trifunovic
Designer: Lorena Susak
Photographer: Rochelle Eagle
Stylist: Jodi Wuestewald
Proofreader: Kaitlyn Smith
Production Director: James Mills-Hicks
Printer: Hang Tai Printing Company Limited

10 9 8 7 6 5 4 3 2 1

OVEN GUIDE: You may find cooking times vary depending on the oven you are using. For fan-forced ovens, as a general rule, set the oven temperature to 20°C (35°F) lower than indicated in the recipe.

Keep up with New Holland Publishers on Facebook
www.facebook.com/NewHollandPublishers